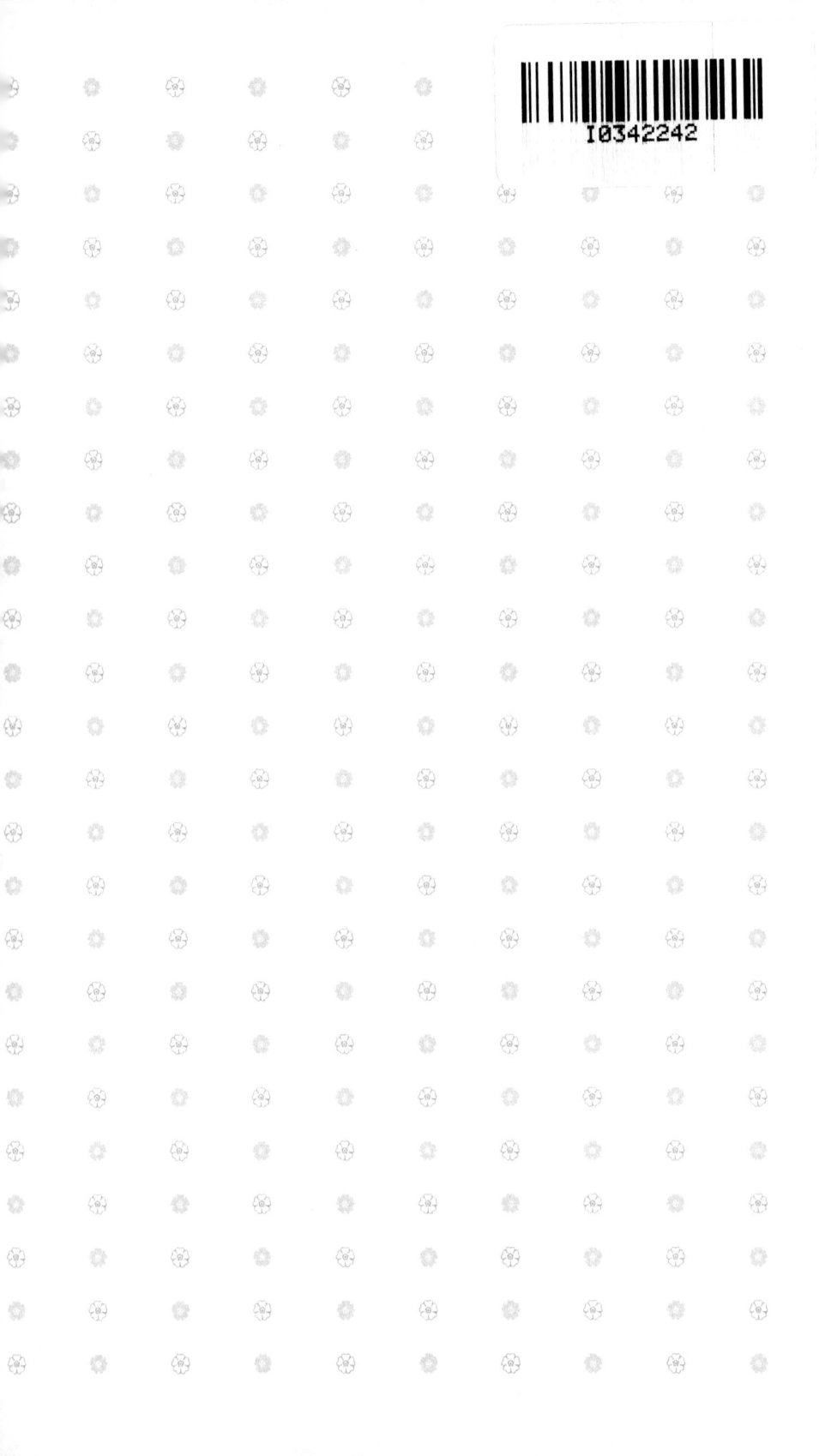

in case of emergency press

We are proud to acknowledge the Traditional Owners of country throughout Australia and to recognise their continuing connection to land, waters, and culture. We pay our respects to their Elders.

We support recognition, reconciliation, and reparation.

Published by in case of emergency press 2023

Copyright © H.T. Grossen 2023

All rights reserved. Without limiting the rights under copyright reserved above, no part of this publication may be reproduced, stored in or introduced into a database and retrieval system or transmitted in any form or any means (electronic, mechanical, photocopying, recording or otherwise) without the prior written permission of both the owner of copyright and the above publishers.

ISBN: 978-0-6456382-8-8

The Long and Short of It

H.T. Grossen

in case of emergency press
https://icoe.com.au
Travancore, Victoria
Australia

About the Author

Henry H.T. Grossen grew up, lives, and writes in the long evening shadow of the Colorado Rocky Mountains. This is his first book of poetry.
For news about upcoming work please visit his website htgrossen.com.
To contact on social media: @htgrossen

This side is

The Long of It

*"Enough!
Waste no more time arguing
what a good man should be.
Be one."*
— Marcus Aurelius

To all the people who have had a hand in shaping my life.
I am thankful for the good times and the bad.
We are bound in love and loss, in blood and dust.

Proverbs 16:3

Table of Contents

65 — Small Town Tales
58 — Ukulele's Birth
50 — Once When I Was a Hero
44 — Speaking with Dale
38 — Floodwater
36 — Twelve Foot Bubble
35 — Hallowed/Hollowed
33 — Blood, Red as Rubies, Her Namesake
28 — Piece of Joy
28 — Mr. Hope
27 — Standard Bearer
27 — Lullabies
27 — Electricity vs Light
25 — Roadrage
24 — Of Searching
23 — Bouquet
23 — High Tower
21 — Bessemer Style
20 — Blood of the Covenant
20 — Water of the Womb
20 — STOP
19 — Insects and Teeth
18 — Therapy
18 — S.C.
18 — a very long yesterday
16 — Chocolat
The Long and Short of It
16 — Carnicero Morales
15 — Highlighter Tears
14 — Welcome to the Zoo
14 — Love, Like a River
14 — Hydrothermal Retrospect

13 — Granny Crosby
13 — Metal Seabird
12 — Reflect
12 — Minority
12 — Sentinel
11 — A Toast During the Zombie Apocalypse
10 — Postmortem
10 — Pearl People - Tom
10 — Pearl People - Donny
10 — Pearl People - Tomahawk
10 — Pearl People - Bobcat
10 — Pearl People - Jimbo
10 — Pearl People - Young Mike
10 — Pearl People - Old Mike
10 — The Pearl Church
9 — Youth
9 — Wheeze Slumps
8 — Narrow, Bottomless
8 — Chasing Butterflies
7 — Patchwork
3 — Haiku Overheard
3 — The Burden of Poets

This is a collection of poems arranged from
longest to shortest.
Some are raw and some are refined, but all are
organized according to line count.
Please feel free to start from either side of the book.

As you read
please adjust your perspective
accordingly.

Small Town Tales

I once fed blind, baby field mice
To a pair of dalmatians
The hairless pink things had been
Found under a woodpile
By brother's gloves
While father split logs
To keep us warm for the winter

I once saw a quarter stick of dynamite
Explode on our property
Throwing fiery pieces of concrete
Into the dry grass
That we stomped out frantically
In panic before laughter caught flame

I once stole a 15 foot tall stop sign
(It has gotten taller as years go by)
Carried it five miles
(The distance has grown as we age)
This decision, fueled by caffeine and boredom
(no alcohol involved, believe it or not)
Was reversed by guilt and we replanted it

I once swam in the irrigation ditch
Beneath a concrete dam
My brother and our friends
Gasped for breath and yelled triumph
Hidden behind a waterfall
Deaf beneath the weight
Of the crop's polluted water

I once spent a day with two marines
We shot a washing machine until it smoked
Fired bullets beneath our feet into a frozen lake
Jumped into the air to do trick shots

The Long and Short of It

With a sawed off shotgun
My hands smelled like cordite for a week
My ears rang for longer

I once sang for a screamo cover band
The bass player didn't show on concert night
So I held the guitar while I sang
Awkwardly plucking half-deaf riffs
That day I learned for the first time
What little talent I truly held

I once saw a car crash
A half mile ahead
The college student had fallen asleep
Ejected beltless from windshield
While the car cartwheeled
Woman ran across highway
To body and tried to straighten
Her broken neck

Now a decade and a half later
A good friend tells me
That stories from small towns are different
Like the one about cousin's father
Sinking a fork deep in his son's flesh
Nailing him Christlike to the oak
Because he reached for a roll
Before grace was over

But more specifically the stories of death:
Cats torn by coyotes
Chicks swallowed by bull snakes
Girl drowning under the floodgates
Young boy whose head was
Caught under father's tractor
Cautionary lunch table talk
Disturbing facts of life
Everyday folktales

Ukulele's Birth

A tangle of purple limbs extracted from my wife's open belly
Cut cord lay upon operating table, slick and green with meconium
Rushing the limp body to a heating table
Swirling blue scrubs say "Vacuum!" terse with added volume
Trembling young nurse opening suction vial after suction vial
Clipping them into hoses fed down her throat straight into her lungs
Her first meal: no mother's milk or warm chest of affection

APGAR of 2. Bad Color. No Reflexes. No respiration.
"Heart rate? Do we have heart rate yet?" "Suction!" "Still not breathing!"

Long ago I saw someone rub a puppy back to life
The only one of the litter who hadn't chosen wobbly steps
Too tired to yowl and find a teat
They simulated the first thrashing gangly stretches that accompany birth
Now experienced head nurse removes rubber gloves
The trick she will perform requiring skin touching skin
Vigorously rubbing my infant's sleeping body
Primal magic called Faith on a level beyond the physical
All of this technology beeping and flashing around us
And it was up to one faceless middle-aged woman
Scrubs, a mask, a hairnet;
To take my child's failing vigor in her hands
And breathe life back into her wrinkled form

You can call it science. You can call it procedure.
What I witnessed that day was a miracle.

Told "stay back" next to my unconscious wife
Blood pooling beneath the table where she lay
It was all going wrong
Then before my eyes: a nurse, and a baby, and God
Made the decision together
My daughter's heart would finally start

Rushing down hidden hallways and up secret elevators
NICU doctors hooked her to machines and wires
I watched long tubes fed into her chest
He wasn't tall but the doctor had kind, tired eyes
That met mine only halfway
When he told me there is a good chance your daughter will make it
But also a chance she won't

Chance is not good, nor is it evil.
It is random, distant, removed from reality.

My daughter's chest vibrated unnaturally
Tiny swollen frame pulsing to a frantic double-kick pedal
Oscillation machine shaking loose polluted lungs
Her body fought infection
Mine a lassitude I could not fathom
Conscious for over 60 hours
Words exited faceless heads and swirled about me
Swallows divebombing an unsuspecting falcon
Pecking against my pounding forehead
Until my torpid consciousness pulled my unmanageable legs
One protracted floor tile at a time, to find and comfort my wife:
Indifferently wheeled into a sterile white room across the building
A heart freshly torn out of her

The oxygen fed down my daughter's nose would keep her alive
Though the pressure in my skull was not to be relieved with sleep
Indecision ever the enemy, I made the only choice available
Although it haunts me still
It doesn't matter that it was only for fifteen minutes:
I left my daughter in a dark room, alone, to be cared for by strangers

Once When I Was a Hero

I pulled a man from
A flaming truck cab
Teeth missing
Blood pouring down his face
From a split scalp
Dripping black in starlight

"I think I left my phone in there
could you get it for me?"

Flames licked the open lips
Of his glove box
Hungry for upholstery
As he had licked salt from the
Final shot glass at 2AM
Hungry for obtundation

"No... It's gone, man."

I made him sit on a cooler
Dislodged from his truck bed
After he split the telephone pole
Voltage dipping dangerously
Close to our heads

"Oh geez... I really need my phone."

The tools of his trade were
Splayed away from us
Far into the field
Across highway lines
Reflecting red and blue
Where firemen and
Paramedics now arrived
Police questioned me

"Did you witness the crash?
What were you doing
when it occurred?"

But I was distracted
Still staring at this man's debris
Littering the ditch
Scattered over there
His carrion wife
Step-kids bloated with potential
A dark shape further out
An apartment, the lease up
Credit card bills tumbleweeding
On winds of disappointment
Hissing pops as his
Engine block cracks

"Back up," the officer urges

I lick sleep-dry lips
Ravenously lapping up irony
As Fire Truck
Extinguishes
fire truck

Speaking with Dale

I was talking with my grandpa
Who passed some years ago
A bright pink evening lit the big living room window
Overlooking over the garden which grandma
Planted, maintained, took joy in

He told me how the squash were doing
The trouble with deer
How to mow the acre just so
A fulltime job in central Illinois
Where the grass grows inches in a day

I forgot the rest, taking conversation for granted
Just like when we spoke when he was alive
It made me miss his quiet strength and vast experience
All the little facts I had learned and forgotten
From him through the years

This was the last time
I would be inside the house he built
So I savored the smells, pattern of the living room ceiling
Softness of the brown living room shag, the texture of my childhood

I thought of my own father
The things he once taught me
I have since forgotten
Whether through carelessness
Or simply time

The fabric of his identity
Tattering and stretching
As my own daughters
Weave thick, rich, colorful personality daily
Learn words, ask questions, rely on me

I choked, "Where does all the time go, Pa?"
He smiled knowingly and looked over grandma's garden
Interlocked his fingers, turned to me sadly, staying silent
As if knowing I would have no time to hear it
And if I did hear him—would I truly listen?

Would it be like other facts he had stated?
Stories Grandma had told, poems my mother recited
Tips for working on cars my father gave me
The strings of life they wove into me that I dyed into my identity
That fade and unravel

As I fade and unravel
As time slips away and I grow old
The blast of an early morning coal train
Pulling me away from the last time
I would ever see my Grandfather in such detail

Floodwater

when the flood came
farmers lost their crop
planted in dirt choked with chemicals
the city's accumulated wealth wiped out
not in an instant
but through days of rising water
slowly drowning cul-de-sacs
homes destroyed: paltry, western, wooden things
soggy drywall so much curdled milk
in the hurricane's irish coffee
they didn't belong
these blackboard chalk homes
erased from the slate with an accidental bump

after the flood
the soil was rich and black again
materialism clung to back yards
like the final frost of spring
rusted bikes and trash bags
melted away
the land was flat
neighborhoods of
dirty trailer homes
reduced to bite size
flecks of aluminum wrapping
swirling in eddies
evaporating

when there are floods in life
rejoice, don't despair
for they are restoration, not destruction
wash the pesticides from your soil
endure the days of rising water
with resolution and consider
if what you own is what brings you life
hurry
before all you hold dear
is swept away
leaving you as you entered
screaming, naked, penniless

Twelve Foot Bubble

My mom had a superpower once
She was radioactive
We weren't supposed to come within
A twelve-foot bubble
While she was undergoing treatment
She lived in the small apartment
Out in the workshop
Alone

She would walk outside after school
My brother and I would sit on the sidewalk
(outside the bubble)
And talk about our day
I remember once
My dad kept walking forward
And the bubble
Popped
-
-
-
-
-
-
-
-
-
-
-
-
He held my mother
Kissed her, the mouth that swallowed
Irradiated pills designed to wither malignancy
That maligned and withered us instead
Said "Stay back, boys"
And took her inside
We smiled, knowing mom would
Heal

Hallowed/Hollowed

Elephants
Have reverence
Deep connections
To their pasts
Careful to step over bones
Feel jaws and sockets
With sensitive trunks
Respecting distant relatives
Souls linked across cosmos
Through ivory and scent

And my buddies
Set off fireworks
In the cemetery
Speak of graverobbing
Laughing
Hoping we don't get haunted
By the ghosts we disturb
Maybe inside rotting casket
Treasure will be found
Gold bar or silver watch
Certainly
The pearly pale
Of loose teeth
Resting in skull

As the elephants
Bow their heads
Peal mournfully for
The spirits in the earth

We drive across town
For 2 AM tacos
They search the desert
For the next watering hole
They say an elephant
Never forgets
But we do

Blood, Red as Rubies, Her Namesake

It was the right thing to do
To keep my family safe
I tied her to a tree

She paced quickly, low to the ground
"It's okay. Sit still. It's okay, girl."
I squeezed the trigger halfway

My ears rang, gunshot pressure cathartic
She yelped, straining, screeching
Not a clean shot

A second bullet
She fell towards me
Twitching

Her tail beat against the dusty ground
In a way that seemed happy
Despite her wild, rolling eyes

Better than my children being attacked
Better than a family unknowingly
Adopting a violent dog

Earlier headache miraculously gone
The cocktail of relief and adrenaline
A fast cure for dread

A single cord of bright crimson splashed
I kicked dirt over the blood
Her namesake: Ruby, now covered

It's curious how substantial a dead animal is
Sheep, ducks, even a mouse feels glutted with death
Twice as heavy dead as she had ever been alive

Her violence, her sharp teeth, her disobedience
Had been transformed
Nothing but meat, fur, and bones

Safe without the threat of violence
Hollow without companionship
A new day dawning on a corpse created

Piece of Joy

Not volcano caused
Or earthquake sized
Not a bomb crater
Broken cobblestones
Wounding the city
No Grand Canyon
No Royal Gorge
Not a rushing fjord

As a child on a hike
In the mountains
I found a crack off the trail
Thin but deep
I dropped a rock inside
And it clattered and echoed
For days, weeks
Down, down, down
Is the rugged heart
My family
Treads upon
This hollow?

You were the size of a thumbnail

When a crack appeared in my heart
A Piece of Joy
Escaped
And my Darling
When we lost you
I knew
I would never get it back

Mr. Hope

He led philosophers
To mountaintops
To scream at God
Both love and frustration

To search is to have hope
But when being lost
Becomes your identity
Where is the promise in that?

Is it a pipe dream
To assume joy
When laboring
9 to 5?

Can we wrap our children with wishes
bind them loosely with vicarious goals
Cash them into the system
Bargaining chips for success?

Is truth a castle in the sky
Something to shake a fist at
On a rocky peak
While it drifts by out of reach?

Aspirations of ambition
Expectation for desire
A dependence on prospects
None amount to much without faith

Bookended with questions
Squeezing him chapbook thin
Pressure flattening the ragged spots
Where he has missing pages

Standard Bearer

Stamping ground, chomping bits
On the eve of battle
A flag flogs the air

Cavalry shakes the Earth
Clouds black with arrows
Hill aflame with blood

What pushes him up the slope towards death?
Summer laughter worth protecting
Meals by a warm hearth

His girls waiting fearfully at home
The desire for future memories
Carries him towards the enemy ranks

How does he swing the sword with leaden arm?
Not just loyalty: this is love
More than friends, his brothers litter the field

If the flag waves the king is still alive
It is protection from the illusion of separation
Assurance the battle can be won

The Standard Bearer
Carried courage for all
Shoulders as wide as the mast

But he lay as sleeping and the flag that fell
As the weary lord fought on
Was picked up by the charging hero

In the midst of chaos
Only a true warrior
Will drop his sword to wave a flag

Lullabies

it's not the pacemaker
that punches the beat
in his heart

i badgered him for months
now a single song
played with blinds drawn

"this is what i sing
for my daughter
before she falls asleep"

strumming once
eyes closed
he is far away

outside himself
more alive than any doctor
could make him

woes forgotten
powerful baritone
eight feet tall

he rocks his baby
with melodies sweet
hands sure

"anyway" the glow fades
from his eyes
unlatches guitar case

this man is not some
middle aged drone
he is lullabies

Electricity vs Light

I used to creep from cave to cave, extinguishing as I went along, doing as I was trained and told. Now, my wife wants every light in the house blazing all day long. It costs about $0.10 to keep a bulb on for 24 hours. You double that for each fixture, then multiply by each switch in the house. Figure you'll have to replace those lights about three times as often, consider inflation and the rising cost of materials. Don't get me started on the chandelier. Factor in children flickering them on and off. Does that really use more electricity? Or did my father, fed up with Charlie's and my attack on any hidden epileptics, tell us that just to get us to stop? I remember it was like blinking– you couldn't tell if your eyelids were moving or not. A brother in motion appearing as a sibling at rest, first on the bed then in the air then on the ground then out the door then in college then walking down the aisle in a tux. Sometimes I blink and I'm already at work despite having just started the car. Other times I blink and I wake up the next morning. I blinked last month and it was our anniversary. I blinked yesterday and my daughter's hair was waist length and bleached from sunshine, but I'm sure she had been hospital bald before I closed my eyes. I know I'm trying to keep my eyes open, toothpicks lodged in tender eyelids, fifteenth cup of coffee turning my stomach, but someone must be flickering the switches because time keeps passing and the speed of light has nothing on these rapid years.

I will say:
She's on to something. It's not about money and it's not about simply keeping the darkness at bay. It's about being present, it's about spending an extra $20 to see, really see your kids grow up.

Roadrage

they swerved like fighting cocks
together and apart
black rubber smoke
throwing gravel at safety rails
middle fingers nearly touching
like two lovers leaning from windows to kiss
speeding down the highway

truck touched SUV
in the resulting seconds
one lurched away
and his middle finger withdrew
to return with a bottle
which dented a door
the other speeding off the exit
to chase the first who threw it

i of course pointed laughing
disbelief on my face
the only other witness: my 2-year-old
i turned to regard her thoughts on her first taste of insanity

she could not see over the dashboard
contented herself with the tops of green trees
blue sky thick with soaring geese
starling murmuration forming Rorschach smiles
a reality only experienced
when we look up

Of Searching

3 AM library silence
moon's wine glass swirl
decimals shining down
alone
in the archive
inquiring after
a long lost thought
a feeling
filed away between
"First Kiss" 300-399
"Last Goodbye" 200-299
not "Nostalgia" 800-899
isn't "Indecision" 100-199
can't be "Cruelty" 900-999
Boolean: bittersweet NOT excruciating
mystery wafts through stacks
like souls
between gravestones
tombs full of
unraveling mycelia
stretching deep into
athenaeum limbo
cemented once again
in my own 499

Bouquet

you'd be almost 6 years old now
knowing life is neither
sunshine nor daisies

but there would be love

pink rose bushes out your bedroom window
a fire in our brick hearth during the first snowfall
catalpa blooms riding morning breezes
baby sisters in tow, laughing
gathering the bounty of the land
fruit of our labor

simple pleasures

it wasn't for those things
you were taken from us
we hope instead
pain, fingertips missing from door jamb
sorrow, dog shuddering final breaths
illness, infections creeping stealing

dry petals dust our windowsill

it hurts so bad
not to know you
squeezing eyes shut
seeing the small condolence
at least you're not hurting worse

High Tower

The two of us
Helped an old woman in an electric wheelchair
Up the stairs to her apartment
Then brought down her old couch
To set on the curb beneath a "Free" sign
I asked her why she lived on the second floor
Why struggle all the time
Why not find a place on the ground level?

She shrugged
"It's a place to live, mi'jito"
I knew what was encoded there:
"I've always been directionless
My family is lost to me
This is my high tower
Where I can keep away
From the problems on the street"

An old CRT wedged into a sunbeam
Pzazzled on
It smelled like hot plastic
Like the fine gear dust
From a worn down box fan
Spinning thanklessly in the corner
Wearily moving stale air for years

Bessemer Style

Cheapest round steak
Weakly brightened by
Orange Manager's Special sticker
Thin and grisly gray
As the man who cooked it

"I'm gonna teach you
How to make a steak
Bessemer Style!
Go bust up that pallet
Behind the dumpster."
A discarded aluminum roasting pan
A grill grate from somewhere
(Possibly "borrowed" from a neighbor's porch)
Chemical pressed palletwood as our fuel
Passed around paper plates
Plastic knives

"Thanks!" said homeless boy to homeless man
"Yeah, thanks," I echoed, an outsider
They take years off the end of life
To stay alive now
Trading health for time

Blood of the Covenant

"Well, shoot.
Done cut my knuckle."
Grandpa shook the hand
Seemingly in no pain at all
Red sprinkled the yellow grass
A chunk of skin stuck
On the end of the tool
He has left little pieces of himself
Here and there
If you look close you can see
A fragment of tooth in the drive
Knee skin on the highway
Blood spatters from here to
The Mississippi River
And back again
Read the palm lines imprinted
Squeezed onto the open hand of my heart:
Toughen up and
Work harder than
Everyone else

Water of the Womb

Parrots echo
Not just words
But noises
My daughter
Wrapped in rainbow down
Wiry growth of full feathers
Poking through
I twirl her
Chiapas dress
Streaming colorful life
She farts
We stop, aghast
Then laugh like
Twin parakeets
Life is too short
For a couple
Cuckoos like us
To care about silly things
Like embarrassment
Or social graces

STOP

Straining in the darkness
Steel slid from black dirt

Ten foot tall sign, two inch steel pipe
Yoked across my shoulders
Bourne two herculean country blocks
As the boys whooped encouragement

Our rebellion soon fizzled into solemn discussion
Of both the legal and social ramifications

See, people drive too fast out here
Not always sober, either

Eight years later Miguel would die
Under a bridge down the road

At a young age we realize
Guilt at the potential for tragedy

We find we need laws
To tame the wilderness within

Though we couldn't yet drive ourselves
We embraced the collective decision
To obey the faded octagon
As the sun rose in the east

Insects and Teeth

Startled awake
By an impatient muse
I am hit with a poem
Dusty moth from a high shelf
Floury fluttering
A memory with silky wings
Soft body
I pinch between my palms
And release into midnight

Other times it's painful
I drill the words from my mouth
Carving away enamel
13,000 RPMs at 110 Volts
Biting down harder and harder
Until I gargle a mouthful of pieces
Panic, regret
Swish, spit
Down the drain
Onto the page

Therapy

No Zoloft no Prozac
No pharmaceuticals at all
Just pick a song of your choosing
A favorite, but nothing too slow
Get in your car
Drive into the country
A little too fast
Roll down your window
Find cows
With the music playing
A little too loud
Scream obscenities at the cattle
As you fly by
And with a cathartic screech
Roll up said window
Go to next song on playlist
Find more bovines
Repeat as needed

S.C.

A conversation we had at work:

"We are all just searching
for our inner Shrek
you know what I mean?"

"I know what you mean, man.
I've just never had the guts to say it!"
We embraced, laughing.

I hope you find your inner Shrek
I hope he's scary and loud but secretly loving
Not a foul-hearted, swamp dwelling monster
When your onion layers are pulled back
With stink and stinging tears
I hope you bleach your black threads
In the light of your father's Father
I hope when you go searching for the occult
You find it
And it scares the bejesus
into you

a very long yesterday

it seemed like a very long yesterday,
Yesterday;
that is to say:
Last Week
which was really:
Last Year,
which was,
now that I think back:
Ten Years Ago.

i have found
with muted distaste
and weary resignation
that children do
in fact
make young women
old
and keep old women
young

Chocolat

White naked beans
Tanned with time and heat
Experienced hands
Playing with fire

Aroma is one thing
Country of Origin another
But did you know
You can tell a good chocolate
By the thickness of the shell?

The thinner the better
More expensive to buy
Richer and easier flavor
It will melt on your tongue
The inside of a master chocolatier's
Truffle is uncomplicated

Much simpler than sex

The Long and Short of It

I could give you reasons
Lamentations and praise
Explain with idioms
And images
Profound

But the long and short of it is this

The people I've met along the way
Have made me into who I am today
I've learned these hard lessons since birth
Known them as truth:

The Long and Short of It

The Golden Rule is not license to be an ass, it is a guideline for self-control.
The effects of this timeless proclamation are to go inward, not outward.
You can try to control others, but you sure can't change them.
Trauma is not a crutch, as society makes it out to be. Trauma is just workout gear:
Carry your heavy burden every day until you realize you are so strong you don't notice it anymore.
The only way to grow is through struggle. I don't make the rules, I just know this one.
Test everything, cling tightly to that which is true. Without truth the flame of your soul will flicker.
Leave every light in your house on, all the time.
Light is life and if you're worried about your bill, just remember:
There is always more money. If you really wanted to, you could get some of it.
If you need to scream at someone (God, spouse, workmate): Please, don't hold it in.
To love is to be vulnerable. An intact heart is a sad thing indeed.
Always tell the truth. Especially when it is hard and
Makes you feel sick to death inside to let it loose upon those you love.

The Long and Short of It

Carnicero Morales

It is said
Faulkner advised
"Kill your darlings"

But the butcher
Trained me to
Cut my children in half
Sew the pretty pieces
Back together
The rest discard: offal and
Broken vestigial limbs

"Keep them alive"
He said
"But only the half
That sounds better.
You'll thank me
Down the road."

Highlighter Tears

Lachrymal Glands
Are what doctors call
Tear ducts

Bright fluid flows through Canaliculi
Emerges salty from Puncta
It is neon green

(yellow and orange
also common colors
when people begin to cry)

Staining tracks fill smile wrinkles
Empathy pinstripes compassionate red cheeks
Dripping emerald onto mothering hands

Frustrating to realize she was
Born to give more love than
She'll ever receive

The Long and Short of It

Welcome to the Zoo

Remember when you could not sleep at night
The day before you took the class field trip to the zoo
Excitement longing yearning
That is how you feel now
At the end of this workday
Not for fun in the sun
But a glass of whiskey in the dark
The giraffe trees you pass on the highway
The anaconda winding river your tires fly over
The sad, swaying elephant chores in a crumbling house
Here you are the animal
With muddled instincts
Wild cravings of a
Mindless beast

Love, Like a River

She smiles in response to his touch
Floodgates of her heart open
Rushing endorphins
Tributary feeding infatuation
The flowing surge of people
Jostle past like so many rolling stones
Trout in the shady places
Hiding beneath the tide of their love

"P.D.A.! Knock that off! Yeecchhh!" I retch loudly
The coupling mouths unlock
I slide quickly downstream
On a current of tepid coffee
To fetch copies, warm and fresh
As the springtime love that fills the hallways

The Long and Short of It

Hydrothermal Retrospect

Grief is deep
Best to remain floating on top
Time, to see through, is crystal
Years each a different shade

Stay in the boat

No diving down for precious memories
Shifting shining stones reflecting reality
Flesh melting off in ribbons prismatic
Old boiling blisters popping, forming anew

Ignore the crescent bands' alluring swindle

Sulfurous in smell
Treacherous breakable crust
Still we like to visit
The rainbow pools

Granny Crosby

My Grandmother does a mean Fanny Crosby
impersonation
If you don't know who that is
She was a missionary who cared for the sick
An artist impassioned by the gospel
Steadily introspective about the condition of her eternal soul
Caring for the impoverished from experience
Her face was a poet's
Skull saturated with verse and rhythm
She wrote poems and composed songs
Her life was a hymn of adventure
Sung by her descendants: actors, illustrators, singers, writers
The unemployed, the alcoholics, the poor, all her people

Fanny did something similar, I think, but she was blind

The Long and Short of It

Metal Seabird

An army of holographic paper cranes
Marches ahead of a veteran
Whose opinions are louder than his Harley
Each one she folds
Reminds her of a day
Her father was not there
A compliment her husband thought
But never said

The polish and stain
Will cover her imperfections
Bleached discolorations, rugged rings of inadequacy
Still exist beneath the surface
Of a life made lonely by choice

Reflect

frozen crystal grown
from ragged edge
dripping sliding catching

fragile emotion
evaporates with heat
intangible pressure

through the withering season
a failed birth
grows into a chance

past wisps
reflected
in present glint

The Long and Short of It

Minority

Her voice cuts through space and time
Frozen ears vibrate, tingle
Waves of range and secret harmonies
Intensifying back to whispers
She is her family, her ancestors
She has her mother's voice
Sings her grandmother's music
Weaving together Europe and South America
Ships of siblings on waves of tradition

Maybe the real minority in this country, she tells me
Are selfless, hard workers
Regardless of color, ethnicity

Sentinel

He stood watch
The wrong way round
Slumping more each day
As is done when age approaches

A gradual return to the earth
Arms to bones to sticks
Eyes to stones to ground
Fission melts away

Once watchful eyes
Puddles of emotion
Forgotten, trodden on
Soaking into the dirt

The Long and Short of It

A Toast During the Zombie Apocalypse

Moans shuffle through thickets
Slim campfire light dances across bark
Alone, separated from my family

Hopeful

My girls are still out there, surviving
I raise the final draught of water
To the black void of night

"To my children if they're zombies
To my children if they're not
Either way I hope they're full of brains
But also full of thoughts"

Postmortem

For years we gave what little we had
To people who had even less
The sides of the scale came up even
Both vessels empty
We gave what was holy to the dogs
We cast our valuable pearls before swine
They trampled us
They turned and they tore us
To pieces and passed us
In piles and slop

Pearl People—Tom

We let a man live in the church
In the back room on a mat
Sober for six months, or so he said
2 AM we get the call, a disturbance
Cops were already there
Empty bottles on the folding chairs
That served as pews
White line of cocaine on a
Black leather cover
The Bible that was a gift to him

Pearl People—Donny

A self-proclaimed bank robber
With too long fingernails
Released from a 35-year sentence
Ivory sheaf of threadlike hair
Comically thick glasses
Jutting chin, no teeth in his top jaw
Lives in an RV, paid cash
Sells tchotchkes out of the back
An entrepreneurial spirit whom you can find
At the flea market to this day

The Long and Short of It

Pearl People—Tomahawk

He would never tell us his name
Just that we should call him Tomahawk
He made copper jewelry   10
(we never asked where he got the wire)
With stones he found in the river
A pet chihuahua
Who rode on his shoulder
As he clung to freight trains
Riding state to state
He disappeared one day

Pearl People—Bobcat

There was a family on the run
Whose mother was gone
And whose father
Let the children choose their own names
I've forgotten them, mostly
But I remember Bobcat
Loved spaghetti
She was creative and wild
Had a soft southern drawl
Poverty made a stereotype of her

The Long and Short of It

Pearl People—Jimbo

A shaking alcoholic hand
Spilling grape juice
From a communion cup   10
Raising it desperately
To his lips
Harmonica in his pocket
Played with passion not skill
His dark house full of warm beer
Always open for an addict to flop
Tears as real as unpaid electric bills

Pearl People—Young Mike

Seventeen & homeless
Known in that part of town
For being the kid who
Spun the Little Caesars board
With flair and an endless smile
Life direction fluttering uncertainly
Arrow pointing up then down then up
Winds of change flipping
Across empty parking lots before soaring
Up into gray clouds laced with silver

Pearl People—Old Mike

Oh, Uncle Mike
What can I say about you
You were one of us
Determined to change
The only one I truly believed in
It sounds cliché
(life is, more often than not)
But addiction is a monster
And its claws were
Too deep inside you

The Pearl Church

We planted a church
Small seed in the bad part of town
We named it The Pearl
A treasure of great value
When we opened our doors
A window was shot out
And a sheet of plywood
Became backdrop of our worship
We endured, watered the seed
With sweat and tears

The Long and Short of It

Youth

I am not aged, just weary
With the great toll life takes

Old enough to know better
Young enough to keep trying anyway

I try to complain about the circumstances I put myself in

But it is a useless sweltering summer breeze, the false hope of relief
That touches the shopping cart figure living under the bridge

Until the day I die there will always be someone saying
"Just wait until you're my age."

Wheeze Slumps

Hallways end in rooms without windows
Bury my head in the
Failing fires in my chest

The neighbors squint at these gut bullets
Coloring grass and asphalt with wheeze slumps
In the growing yards between us

Oily, mouth drops burning pearlescent discharge
With neon chills, sweat sleeps now
For every second dies, and must

The Long and Short of It

Chasing Butterflies

Rough trunk galls
Abandoned bird nests
Water-skaters ripple
Ants move eggs in blinding rock flips
Humming wings bellicose and blue spotted
A pine needle tangled in pink braids
Wild onion blooms trick young noses
Painful lessons in tree climbing

Narrow, Bottomless

Mountain soil
Wealth
Brushing pine
Rocks encircled
Hand spade
Fingers never
To hold, to scold

We buried a heart shaped box and wept 'neath splitting gray skies

The Long and Short of It

Patchwork

Barely my knowledge suffices
Pieces tanglewhipped together
To a self-pity tree
Guilt trembling fingers
Weave a rope of lies:
The lynchpin of another failed plan

My demise singularly my own

Haiku Overheard

3   "You're not black, man!"
    "Oh yeah? My step-dad is black.
    That means I'm step-black!"

The Long and Short of It

The Burden of Poets

I cleverly call it "The Writer's Curse"
The author and I touch cans together and laugh
Though I know Alcoholism isn't a joke

This is a collection of poems arranged from
shortest to longest.
Some are raw and some are refined, but all are
organized according to line count.
Please feel free to start from either side of the book.

As you read
please adjust your perspective
accordingly.

18 — a very long yesterday
18 — S.C.
18 — Therapy
19 — Insects and Teeth
20 — STOP
20 — Water of the Womb
20 — Blood of the Covenant
21 — Bessemer Style
23 — High Tower
23 — Bouquet
24 — Of Searching
25 — Roadrage
27 — Electricity vs Light
27 — Lullabies
27 — Standard Bearer
28 — Mr. Hope
28 — Piece of Joy
33 — Blood, Red as Rubies, Her Namesake
35 — Hallowed/Hollowed
36 — Twelve Foot Bubble
38 — Floodwater
44 — Speaking with Dale
50 — Once When I Was a Hero
58 — Ukulele's Birth
65 — Small Town Tales

Table of Contents

3 — The Burden of Poets
3 — Haiku Overheard
7 — Patchwork
8 —Narrow, Bottomless
8 — Chasing Butterflies
9 — Wheeze Slumps
9 — Youth
10 — The Pearl Church
10 — Pearl People - Old Mike
10 — Pearl People - Young Mike
10 — Pearl People - Jimbo
10 — Pearl People - Bobcat
10 — Pearl People - Tomahawk
10 — Pearl People - Donny
10 — Pearl People - Tom
10 — Postmortem
11 — A Toast During the Zombie Apocalypse
12 — Sentinel
12 — Minority
12 — Reflect
13 — Metal Seabird
13 — Granny Crosby
14 — Hydrothermal Retrospect
14 — Love, Like a River
14 — to the Zoo
15 — Highlighter Tears
16 — Carnicero Morales
The Long and Short of It
16 — Chocolat

To:
My God
My Family
Southeast Colorado

Prov. 16:3

This side is

The Short of It

"The truth is something that burns."
Jordan Peterson

A little about the Author

H.T. Grossen lives in Pueblo, CO.
This is his first book of poetry.
Social media: @htgrossen
Web: htgrossen.com.

The Long and
Short of It

H.T. Grossen

in case of emergency press
https://icoe.com.au
Travancore, Victoria
Australia

in case of emergency press

We are proud to acknowledge the Traditional Owners of
country throughout Australia and to recognise their
continuing connection to land, waters, and culture.
We pay our respects to their Elders.

We support recognition, reconciliation, and reparation.

Published by in case of emergency press 2023

Copyright © H.T. Grossen 2023
All rights reserved.

ISBN: 978-0-6456382-8-8

www.ingramcontent.com/pod-product-compliance
Lightning Source LLC
Chambersburg PA
CBHW020329010526
44107CB00054B/2041